Volleyball

BY M. K. OSBORNE

AMICUS | AMICUS INK

Amicus High Interest is published by Amicus and Amicus Ink
P.O. Box 1329, Mankato, MN 56002
www.amicuspublishing.us

Library of Congress Cataloging-in-Publication Data
Names: Osborne, M. K., author.
Title: Volleyball / by M. K. Osborne.
 Description: Mankato, Minnesota : Amicus, [2020] |
Series: Summer Olympic sports | Includes bibliographical
 references and index. | Audience: Grade 4 to 6.
Identifiers: LCCN 2019005911 (print) | LCCN 2019006793
 (ebook) | ISBN 9781681518664 (pdf) | ISBN
 9781681518268 (library binding) | ISBN
 9781681525549 (pbk.)
Subjects: LCSH: Volleyball–Juvenile literature. | Olympics–
Juvenile literature.
Classification: LCC GV1015.34 (ebook) | LCC GV1015.34
.O64 2020 (print) | DDC 796.325–dc23
LC record available at https://lccn.loc.gov/2019005911

Editor: Wendy Dieker
Designer: Aubrey Harper
Photo Researcher: Shane Freed

Photo Credits: Jeff Roberson/AP cover; Fotoarena/Alamy 4,
16–17, 20; Hulton Archive/Stringer/Getty 7; Gan-Shmuel
archive via the PikiWiki – Israel free image collection project/
WikiMedia Commons 8; Pedro Ugarte/Getty 11; Anonymous/
AP 12; Marcio Jose Sanchez/AP 15; Leon Neal/Getty 19;
Bob Galbraith/AP 23; PCN Black/Alamy 24; Marcelo Del
Pozo/Newscom 26; Johannes Eisele/Getty 28–29

Printed in the United States of America

HC 10 9 8 7 6 5 4 3 2 1
PB 10 9 8 7 6 5 4 3 2 1

Table of Contents

Going for Gold

It's **match point**. The setter launches the ball up. Spike! The hitter slams the ball to the floor on the other side of the net. It's a win! The crowd goes wild! This is Olympic volleyball. Every four years, the best volleyball players in the world meet on the court. They all want a gold medal. Who will win?

Olympic volleyball features amazing athletes and high-action games.

A Fun New Game

Volleyball is an old game. In 1895, William G. Morgan invented it. He wanted a sport that was easy and fun for his gym class. He raised up a tennis net. The class was split into two teams. The players used their hands to **volley** a ball back and forth over the net. The game was a hit!

People of all ages play
volleyball. These kids play
on an outdoor court.

Men's teams from Israel and the Soviet Union play in the 1952 world championship game.

Q What does FIVB stand for?

Soon this new game spread to Europe. In 1947, the **FIVB** formed. It is a group that makes the rules for world games. Two years later, the FIVB hosted the first volleyball world championship games. Teams from around Europe played to win. Volleyball would soon be an Olympic sport.

 It is short for the French term Fédération Internationale de Volleyball. In English, it is the International Volleyball Federation.

Volleyball has simple rules. One team **serves** the ball over the net. The other team gets three hits to knock the ball back over. If the ball hits the ground on their side, the other team scores.

Players will use the first two hits to set up powerful spikes. These smashing hits can zoom at 80 miles per hour (129 km/h)!

 What is a game called in volleyball?

A player serves the ball to start a volley.

 Games are called matches. Matches are made of three or five sets. The team that wins the most sets wins the match.

In the 1964 Olympics, the U.S. women battle the home team in Japan.

Olympic Indoor Volleyball

The first Olympic indoor volleyball games were held in 1964. Ten men's teams and six women's teams faced off. The Japanese women thrilled their fans. They won all five of their matches. They won the gold medal. The Soviet Union's men's team won eight of their nine matches. They claimed the men's gold medal.

Today, the Olympics features 12 men's and 12 women's indoor teams. Country teams battle in tournaments leading up to the Summer Games. The top teams get to compete at the Olympics.

The teams are split into two pools. The top four teams in each pool play to win a medal. The team that wins all their matches takes the gold medal.

An official Olympic indoor volleyball is about 25 inches (63.5 cm) around.

At the Olympics, teams must win three sets to win the match. If a team wins three in a row, the match is over. Olympic volleyball often is a game of comebacks. A team might lose the first two sets. And then they come back to win the next two. Fans cheer hard for their team in the fifth set. Who will win?

Blockers from Brazil jump to stop a big spike from Japan in a 2016 Olympic match.

Beach Volleyball

You might think the beach is for relaxing. But that's where you will find more volleyball action. Casual games of volleyball on the beach have turned into serious competitions. The basics of beach volleyball are the same as indoor games. But there are only two players on a team. It is a game of quickness and teamwork.

Sand flies as Bárbara Seixas de Freitas of Brazil dives for the ball duing a 2016 Olympic match.

Fans fill the beach volleyball arena in Rio de Janeiro during the 2016 Olympics.

Q What is a **demo sport**?

Beach volleyball was a demo sport in the 1992 Olympics. Fans loved the fast-paced action. Players flew around the court. They dove to get the **dig**. They spun around to set up a spike. They flew in the air for the big spike. In beach volleyball, players can't focus on just one area of the game. They must be able to do it all very well.

 It's an event to show the crowds what the sport is like. If fans like the sport, it might become an official event.

Beach volleyball became an Olympic sport in 1996. Twenty-four men's teams and 18 women's teams hit the sand. U.S. indoor volleyball stars Charles "Karch" Kiraly and Kent Steffes won the men's gold.

Today, there are spots for 24 men's and women's teams. Teams **qualify** based on their winnings in tournaments leading up to the Olympics.

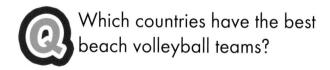 Which countries have the best beach volleyball teams?

Two U.S. men's teams played in the first Olympic gold-medal match in 1996.

 Brazil and the United States. They have won medals in every Summer Games.

Like indoor play, teams are put into pools. They play matches to qualify for the medal tournament. The team that wins two of three sets wins the match.

Two countries have teams that dominate the medal stand. Brazil has won the most medals overall. But the U.S. leads with the most gold medals.

Players from the U.S. and Brazil meet at the net in the quarter-final match in 2016.

Misty May-Treanor (left) and Kerri Walsh Jennings celebrate a point in the 2012 Olympics.

Q Do May-Treanor and Jennings still play together?

The beach is where volleyball's stars are made. The U.S. team of Misty May–Treanor and Kerri Walsh Jennings is called one of the greatest teams ever. These two women earned gold medals in 2004, 2008, and 2012. They lost only one Olympic set. They won all 21 matches those years.

 No. May-Treanor retired after the 2012 Olympics. Jennings found a new teammate. They won a bronze medal in 2016.

Olympic Glory

Fans can't get enough of the volleyball action at the Olympics. Whether on the court or at the beach, it's a thrilling sport. So kick back and watch your nation's teams. Cheer as the best bump, set, and spike their way to Olympic glory.

The U.S. women's indoor team celebrates winning a bronze medal in 2016.

Glossary

demo sport A sport that is played for show; players do not earn medals if they win.

dig A play in which a player saves a hard shot from hitting the ground.

FIVB In French, it is short for Fédération Internationale de Volleyball, which is the International Federation of Volleyball. This group makes the rules for international volleyball games.

match point A point in a volleyball game that will win the match for a team.

qualify To earn a spot in a sporting competition.

serve To start a volley by hitting the ball over the net from the back of the court.

volley To hit a ball back and forth.

Read More

Kortemeier, Todd. *12 Reasons to Love Volleyball.* Mankato, Minn.: 12-Story Library, 2018.

McIntyre, Abigael. *An Insider's Guide to Volleyball.* New York: Rosen Central, 2015.

Peters, Stephanie True. *Great Moments in the Summer Olympics.* New York: Little, Brown and Co., 2012.

Websites

Beach Volleyball | Olympic.org
www.olympic.org/beach-volleyball

The Game | International Volleyball Federation
www.fivb.org/thegame/TheGame_Volleyball OlympicGames.htm

Volleyball | Olympic.org
www.olympic.org/volleyball

Index

About the Author

M. K. Osborne is a children's writer and editor who gets excited about the Olympics, both the Summer and Winter Games, every two years. Osborne pores over stats and figures and medal counts to bring the best stories about the Olympics to young readers.